A Fresh Start:

Steps to Spiritual Renewal

Tom Foley

Christian Educators Outreach
Charlottesville, Virginia

Completed by _____

Date _____

A Fresh Start: Steps to Spiritual Renewal
Copyright © 2020 Thomas L. Foley
All rights reserved.
ISBN: 978-0-9990542-5-3

This book is a ministry resource published by
Christian Educators Outreach to help followers of Jesus
as they pray, think and grow in their in personal discipleship.
The views expressed are those of the author and not necessarily those of
Christian Educators Outreach, its Board of Directors or its employees.

Christian Educators Outreach
Charlottesville, Virginia
www.ceokids.org

Scripture quotations are from the ESV® Bible
(The Holy Bible, English Standard Version®)
copyright © 2001 by Crossway,
a publishing ministry of Good News Publishers.
Used by permission. All rights reserved.
ESV Text Edition: 2016

DEDICATION

…to the scores of people who have traveled with me through the last
decades of walking as fellow-disciples,
learning together about disciple-making,
all the while seeking a deeper understanding of our Lord
and the task laid before us by him.

Nothing is perfect, except God, and certainly not this book.
While scores of people had input on this edition from using earlier editions,
all the mistakes you find are mine.
Please don't be deterred by errors, but move into renewal.

– Tom Foley

AUTHOR'S PREFACE:

HOW TO USE THIS RESOURCE

This book is a self-guided resource to strengthen your personal discipleship, or if you prefer, spiritual development. No matter how long you have been following Jesus, I believe this book will help you on your journey. Here are some clues on how to best use this resource. You may wish to skip around. However, experience tells me that the most effective use is to proceed in order.

In every case, follow your 'gut' (that is, your first instinct). For the disciple of Jesus our 'gut' is often a way that God may speak to us. Take your first reaction and go with it. Write it down before you overthink it. After which, you can think and modify as much as you find necessary and helpful.

The resource has three parts. Part One is about looking back and in. Part Two is about looking forward. Part Three contains some 'tools' to help you keep moving in your personal discipleship. I suggest that you begin the way we do up in the mountains: Set aside 3-4 hours in solitude, get out your previous 12 months of calendar(s), turn off your phone, have some refreshments within reach and begin. The booklet assumes that you will be considering twelve months, but any period of time works in this kind of reflection.

As you work your way through Part One, if a question has no ready answer, write the first thing that comes to mind and keep writing. It may take you a few minutes to get in the swing of things, but set your mind to it, pray and press on. All along the way, ask our loving Father to help you and move forward. This process may not be easy - meaningful things seldom are. When you finish Part One take a break to stretch, have a sip of water and get a breath of fresh air. It will help the functioning of your brain.

In Part Two you will look ahead. Just like in Part One, pray, trust your gut, and keep writing. The more you write, the more your brain will make connections, and God will help you concentrate on looking forward. If you can't finish in the time you've allotted, come back to it as soon as you can. Stick with it.

For married couples, when possible, we suggest each person work through the questions and exercises on their own and then sit together to discuss and compare notes and unite on objectives. Then, the couple could collaborate on the plans that go with the objectives. In this way your fresh start rightfully goes from your relationship with God to your relationship with your most beloved human.

When you finish, go back to the cover page and fill in your name and date of completion to show that YOU are the final author of this work. (We've included several blank pages at the end of this book to give you extra space if you need it for any answers or exercises.

Final advice: Relax… Begin with a heart that is open and rested. That means to get good night's sleep the night before, ask God to guide the process and enjoy! And remember:

NO GUILT, NO SHAME!
There is no condemnation
for those of us in Christ Jesus!
(from Romans 8:1)

Tom Foley
Charlottesville, Virginia
April, 2020

CONTENTS

PART ONE - LOOK BACK AND INWARD

Set Your Mind   3

Looking Back   7

Reflect   13

Gratitude   17

Looking Deeper   19

PART TWO - PRACTICAL STEPS FORWARD

Looking Ahead   33

Praying Forward   43

Celebrate   47

PART THREE - FURTHER RESOURCES

Spiritual Disciplines   51

Bible Meditation   61

A Sailboat Metaphor   63

M'Cheyne Bible Reading Plan   67

PART ONE

*Don't look back with regret,
Or at present circumstances with fear,
But forward, in faith,
Trusting God.*

1

"SET YOUR MIND…"

Let's begin by looking to Scripture to get our heart and mind ready for what lies ahead.

Read through slowly and prayerfully to prepare your heart.

Set your minds on things that are above, not on things that are on earth. Colossians 3:2

To you I lift up my eyes, O you who are enthroned in the heavens! Psalm 123:1

Be exalted, O God, above the heavens! Let your glory be over all the earth! Psalm 57:5

But you, O Lord, are a God merciful and gracious, slow to anger and abounding in steadfast love and faithfulness. Turn to me and be gracious to me; give your strength to your servant, and save the son of your maidservant. Show me a sign of your favor, that those who hate me may see and be put to shame because you, LORD, have helped me and comforted me. Psalm 86:15-17

For you, O LORD, are most high over all the earth; you are exalted far above all gods. Psalm 97:9

Not to us, O Lord, not to us, but to your name give glory, for the sake of your steadfast love and your faithfulness! Psalm 115:1

O Lord, our Lord, how majestic is your name in all the earth! Psalm 8:9

Lord, you have been our dwelling place in all generations. Before the mountains were brought forth, or ever you had formed the earth and the world, from everlasting to everlasting you are God. Psalm 90:1-2

I will greatly rejoice in the LORD; my soul shall exult in my God, for he has clothed me with the garments of salvation; he has covered me with the robe of righteousness. Isaiah 61:10

Come to me, all who labor and are heavy laden, and I will give you rest. Take my yoke upon you, and learn from me, for I am gentle and lowly in heart, and you will find rest for your souls. For my yoke is easy, and my burden is light. Matthew 11:28-30

God is our refuge and strength, a very present help in trouble. Psalm 46:1

Trust in the LORD with all your heart, and do not lean on your own understanding. Proverbs 3:5

Stand therefore, having fastened on the belt of truth, and having put on the breastplate of righteousness, and, as shoes for your feet, having put on the readiness given by the gospel of peace. In all circumstances take up the shield of faith, with which you can extinguish all the flaming darts of the evil one; and take the helmet of salvation, and the sword of the Spirit, which is the word of God, praying at all times in the Spirit, with all prayer and supplication. To that end keep alert with all perseverance, making supplication for all the saints,… Ephesians 6:14-18

Whoever listens to me will dwell secure and will be at ease, without dread of disaster. Proverbs 1:33

Bless the LORD, O my soul! O LORD my God, you are very great! You are clothed with splendor and majesty, covering yourself with light as with a garment, stretching out the heavens like a tent. Psalm 104:1-2

Blessed is the man who trusts in the LORD, whose trust is the LORD. He is like a tree planted by water, that sends out its roots by the stream, and does not fear when heat comes, for its leaves remain green, and is not anxious in the year of drought, for it does not cease to bear fruit. Jeremiah 17:7-8

As a father shows compassion to his children, so the LORD shows compassion to those who fear him. For he knows our frame; he remembers that we are dust. Psalm 103:13-14

The steadfast love of the LORD never ceases; his mercies never come to an end; they are new every morning; great is your faithfulness. Lamentations 3:22-23

Though the fig tree should not blossom, nor fruit be on the vines, the produce of the olive fail and the fields yield no food, the flock be cut off from the fold and there be no herd in the stalls, yet I will rejoice in the LORD; I will take joy in the God of my salvation. GOD, the Lord, is my strength; he makes my feet like the deer's; he makes me tread on my high places. Habakkuk 3:17-19

Let the righteous one rejoice in the LORD and take refuge in him! Let all the upright in heart exult! Psalm 64:10

2

LOOKING BACK

"By this my Father is glorified, that you bear much fruit and so prove to be my disciples. As the Father has loved me, so have I loved you. Abide in my love." John 15:8-9

Jesus looked for fruit in the lives of his disciples. As his disciples, we should stop and look back periodically to check our fruit. But looking back should not cause discouragement or create guilt. When you look back, the most important thing is to see life in the light of the gospel. As you stop and look back, the objective is to gain important insight into what is inside.

The steps on the pages that follow are designed to help you look back, inward, and then forward as we journey with Jesus. Don't rush, but neither should you drag your feet. As you go through the steps, learn to trust your instincts (also known as your 'gut', or first reaction). This is your exercise, so feel free to skip questions. (But you might find that, later, you can go back with an answer!) During the next couple of hours, continue to pray and work through the steps of this exercise.

You might begin with this prayer:

"Loving Father, as I look back, inside, around and ahead, please use your Spirit to show me what YOU want me to see. Please remind me of what is important. Please help me to see those people whom I need to love better. Please show me that you are always with me and that in Christ I am not condemned. Please guide my objectives and plans. In all of this, may you receive glory, and may my plans be from YOU. In the great name of Jesus, I ask, Amen."

LOOK BACK

Now, take a while and look back through your planner / calendar of the last 12 months (the length of time is up to you). Use the blank pages that follow to write notes, draw diagrams, charts, graphs, or whatever helps you make a record for yourself of the time just past. This could be a year, a season or the period since an important event (like a move or job change). Take time to recall the significant events, meaningful experiences and the memories and emotions of this period of time, whether good or not-so-good. Especially consider events that had spiritual, emotional, physical, family and professional impact.

A page for your notes.

Another page for your notes.

Yet another page for your notes.

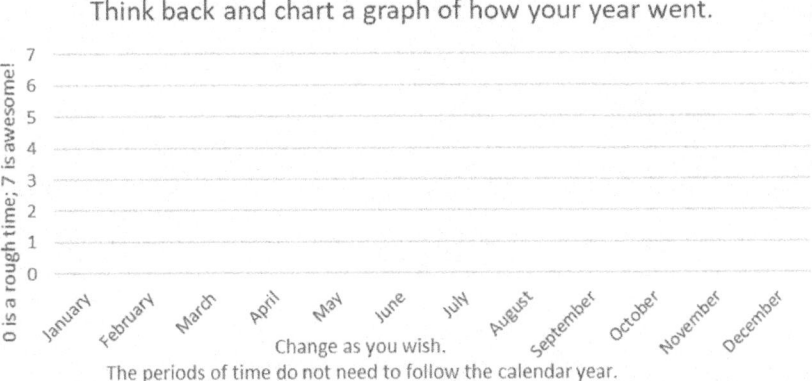

Think back and chart a graph of how your year went.

3

REFLECT

Now, based on your review of last year, think through the following:

1. What was/were significant family event(s)?

2. What was/were significant marital event(s)?

3. What was/were significant professional event(s)?

4. What was/were memorable spiritual event(s)?

5. Which one word best describes your physical health?

6. How did you grow intellectually (through reading, study, film or conversation)?

7. How would you describe your emotional life?

8. Keeping in mind the Greatest Commandment (Mark 12:28-34): How did you grow in your love for your Heavenly Father?

9. How did you grow in loving people?

10. What person or persons had a positive influence on you last year?

11. On whom did you have a positive impact?

12. On whom would you like to have had a positive impact?

13. What event(s) of the last 12 months significantly affected the direction of your life?

14. Who was the person/persons that you struggled most with last year? What should you do about that? Are you making progress in this/these relationships?

15. Who is that person you still need to forgive?

16. What did you learn from the use of spiritual disciplines last year? (There is a description of some disciplines beginning on page 51.)

17. What surprised you about last year?

18. What were your biggest answered prayers?

19. Describe your disciple-making in the last 12 months.

20. What 3 or 4 words describe your year?

21. Make note of four things that you want to improve on from last year (or whatever period of time). This is important for Part 2.

4
GRATITUDE

Now that you've looked back, STOP AND THANK GOD!

Briefly look back over those last pages and, in the space that follows, write a prayer of thanksgiving.

Remember: We can, and should, be thankful in the struggles as well as the victories.

"...give thanks in all circumstances..." (1 Thess. 5:18)

5

LOOKING DEEPER

"And we all, with unveiled face, beholding the glory of the Lord, are being transformed into the same image from one degree of glory to another. For this comes from the Lord who is the Spirit." 2 Corinthians 3:18

Now that you've completed your scan of the past year and practiced some gratitude, it's time to dig a bit deeper. Read, think and pray through the following questions and write out your answers as vulnerably and honestly as you are able. For some of the questions, rather than writing an answer, you can think about things using a spectrum.

X marks the spot!

The various spectrums on the following pages are designed to get you thinking. After thinking about them, mark X on the spectrum, like this:

|--X---------------|

SPIRITUAL DEVELOPMENT

The first topic explores your personal investment with God in your own spiritual development (not ministry). Begin by slowly reading 2 Peter 1:3-7.

> His divine power has granted to us all things that pertain to life and godliness, through the knowledge of him who called us to his own glory and excellence, by which he has granted to us his precious and very great promises, so that through them you may become partakers of the divine nature, having escaped from the corruption that is in the world because of sinful desire. For this very reason, make every effort to supplement your faith with virtue, and virtue with knowledge, and knowledge with self-control, and self-control with steadfastness, and steadfastness with godliness, and godliness with brotherly affection, and brotherly affection with love.

1. Peter lists several characteristics of a godly life (faith, virtue, knowledge, self-control, steadfastness, godliness, brotherly affection, and love). Which of these would you like to see more of in your personal growth in the next 12 months? Circle or underline the ones you would like to see increase in your life.

faith
virtue
knowledge
self-control
steadfastness
godliness
brotherly affection
love

2. As you look back over your reflections, think about emotions, what emotions stand out?

3. In what ways do those emotions reflect past growth?

4. In what ways do those emotions show your need for future growth?

5. List the emotions that you struggled with in the last year.

6. How would your spouse (or your parents, your closest friend) agree or disagree with your responses to the last questions about your emotions?

7. Who is that person that you still need to forgive from the past year (or beyond)?

Now, take a moment or two and pray about the last few questions. If forgiveness is an issue for you in any respect, pause and pray by name for those damaged relationships. Confess your unforgiveness to God and ask him to help you forgive and wish the best for that unforgiven person(s).

Remember: On the cross, Jesus said "It is finished."
Our sin is PAID FOR!

SITTING WITH GOD

Calvin described prayer as climbing into the lap of God, reading the Bible can be steps to his throne of grace.

On average, how many days per week do you spend time with God to...

Read Scripture

|---|
1   2   3   4   5   6   7

Pray

|---|
1   2   3   4   5   6   7

Listen to God

|---|
1   2   3   4   5   6   7

Which phrase best describes your Bible reading time?

|---|

a chore   a duty   a joy when I do it   best part of my day!

How would you like for your time with God to improve? Finish this sentence: I would like for my time with God to improve in the area of...

And to do that, I am willing to...

WALKING WITH FELLOW-DISCIPLES
(DISCIPLE-MAKING)

1. In the Spiritual Development Section (above), you may have found areas in which you would like to make some progress. With whom are you vulnerable and honest in discussing the areas you have just been thinking about?

2. Have you been vulnerable and honest with that/those person(s) lately?

3. How often do you think you need to meet with this/these person(s)?
|--|
Never   Yearly   Monthly   Every 2 weeks   Weekly

4. How often do you actually meet with this/these person(s)?
|--|
Seldom   Sometimes   Regularly

5. What information have you held back from that person? About what might you stop and talk with God about right now?

MARRIAGE

While working on our marriage is not easy, it is the most important human relationship we will ever have. So, think about your marriage.

1. What would you and your spouse (you'll have to guess) say were the high points over the last year?

	HIGH POINTS	LOW POINTS
YOU		
HIM OR HER		

2. For what might you need to seek or offer forgiveness?

3. If you were to write your autobiography of the last year, what parts of it would surprise your spouse because you have not shared them with him/her? Why?

4. What are three ways you would like your marriage to progress in the coming year?

5. What three actions can you take that you know will improve your marriage?

HEALTH

*Let's take care of this temple (1 Corinthians 6:19)
so that we are ready for His use!*

Think about your health and the practices that affect it.

1. Eating habits:
|---|
Terrible   Stuck   Improving   Improved   On Target

2. Exercise:
|---|
Terrible   Making Excuses   Improving   Better!   On Track

3. Weekly Sabbath:
|---|
Never   Seldom   Sometimes   Often   Weekly

4. Sleep:
|---|
Insomniac   Fitful   Not Enough   Okay   Plenty

45 minutes of cardio exercise 5 times a week can repair your brain as well as improve your general health!

5. What health goal would you like to achieve this year?

By when?

Who will help you with this goal?

6. What health problem in your life remains undealt with?

7. What sort of health maintenance would be helpful to your overall well-being? Regular exercise? More care in eating habits? Ample sleep? A day off? A vacation?

8. What kind of recreation brings you joy? (Feeling content, smiling and/or laughter can sometimes be good signs.)

7. How often do you pursue activities that bring you joy?
|--|
Never   Seldom   Sometimes   Often

8. According to your own experience, how important are family and friends to your well-being?
|--|
Little   Sort of   Very   Essential

9. How often do you make time for family and friends?
|--|
Never   Seldom   Sometimes   Often

10. How would you like to see the aspects of joy, family and friendship change in your life?

Congratulations! You're making great progress. Keep at it!

YOUR PROFESSION

Whether homemaker, student, pastor, manager or office worker, this section will cause you to think about an area of life to which you devote many hours. (If you're primarily a student, consider your studies your job.)

Soli Deo Gloria!
To God be all the glory in every aspect of our lives, including our work!

1. Overall, in your job over the last year, were you … ?
|--|
Discouraged   Encouraged   Excited

2. How often do you experience joy in your work?
|--|
Never   Seldom   Sometimes   Often   Usually

3. In your job over the last year, what were the events that blessed you?

4. What are the ways you were frustrated?

5. If money were no object, into what kind of work would you invest your life's energy, effort and time?

6. Consider the previous answer, how similar is what you are doing to what you just wrote about?

|--|
Not at all   Sort of   Pretty much   Just like it!

7. How much do you think about your work as being essential to your personal discipleship, or as part of God's kingdom (this includes all kinds of work).

|--|
Never   Seldom   Sometimes   Often   Usually

8. As you consider the last 2 pages of questions, what do your answers tell you about the way that you could be praying about the professional aspect of your life?

*Remember when we look back,
ultimately, we want to see the cross and
the finished work of Jesus more than anything else.*

OVERALL

Read the description of the sail/row/drift/sink metaphor beginning on **page 63.**

Would you say you are:

|--|
Sinking   Drifting   Rowing   Sailing

REMEMBER: There is no condemnation
for those who are
IN CHRIST JESUS!!! (from Romans 8:1)

CONGRATULATIONS!

You have looked back and in. So, take a 10-minute break, get something to drink, get some fresh air, and stretch. This will refresh your brain, so you can move into Part Two! Stretching gets the blood moving through your muscles and that fresh blood movement gets fresh blood into your brain. Also, if you're just a little dehydrated, it lessens the functioning power of your brain. Stand up, stretch, go for a brief walk and be glad about the progress you've made!!!

PART TWO

6

LOOKING AHEAD

Now that you've had a break, take one more look back at what you've written about the past year. Try to answer any questions you skipped. Take a highlighter or a different color pen and go back through the previous pages. Highlight or put stars, smiley faces, frowns, or other marks on the pages as you identify some of the changes you would like to see. Write some (or all) of those changes here:

Now that you've finished looking back…

Pray this prayer: "Father, thank you for time past. Help me not feel any condemnation but rather, help me be thankful, and may I look to you so that I may move forward in your strength and direction. Be glorified in my life as I pray in Jesus name, Amen."

You've invested time in looking back, some looking in, it's time to look ahead. This stage is about setting some objectives and goals.

Jesus said: "But whoever would be great among you must be your servant, and whoever would be first among you must be your slave, even as the Son of Man came not to be served but to serve, and to give his life as a ransom for many." Matthew 20:26b-28

Write the name of one or two persons that you could intentionally serve in the next 12 months.

What new or renewed spiritual disciplines will you focus upon in the coming months? (See the list of the disciplines beginning on page 51).

HINTS ON SETTING OBJECTIVES

Helpful objectives are:

- Attainable (Hint: If you've never run a 5k, it may not be wise to start with a marathon.)
- Measurable (Example: I will take my wife out to a place of her choosing once every month for the next 12 months.)
- Realistic, but still a stretch (Example: I'll read the M'Cheyne Bible reading plan 4-6 days per week.)
- Specific (Example: I will meet with fellow-disciples twice a month to grow in Christ through conversation and Scripture reading.)
- Flexible. (Example: If, after 3 months, you and your fellow disciple(s) see that your "run 10 miles" objective is unattainable, set a more reasonable goal that can be achieved. There's no shame in being flexible.).

Remember these objectives are for YOU, not to impress someone else. Establish objectives that will help you on your path to being a better servant of God. "For by the grace given to me I say to everyone among you not to think of himself more highly than he ought to think, but to think with sober judgment, each according to the measure of faith that God has assigned." (Rom 12:3)

Now, move forward! On the next pages set some objectives. It might be helpful to think about one for spiritual development, one for marriage and family, one for health, or one for work. This is only a suggestion! Don't feel constrained by this suggestion, it is just to get you thinking. You don't need to fill up the page as you'll be returning to these objectives in the next section to add steps toward reaching your objective.

Now, take a few moments to pause and pray; ask your heavenly Father to guide you through the objective setting section.

(There is a page for each objective because there are additional steps that will bring you back to these four pages to use the objectives to make plans.)

This year, by God's Grace, I will…

This year, by God's Grace, I will…

This year, by God's Grace, I will…

This year, by God's Grace, I will…

STEPS TOWARD YOUR OBJECTIVES

Well Done!!! You've just done something that many, many people will never do. But it's been said that an objective without a deadline is no objective at all.

- Before the next step, it is important to assign some dates. So, *go back* to the objectives and assign a date. Some objectives can't really be dated, so in that case, set a date to reevaluate.

- Now that you've set some objectives, you need to make some plans to achieve those objectives. Every journey has steps, twists, turns, and stages. Go to each of the objectives you've set and think about practical changes you can make to see that they become a reality. (Example: get up 30 minutes before my spouse to make time for God.) Go back to the previous pages where you've set your objectives and write down the steps needed to make progress toward your objectives.

- Perhaps discussing this with a group of fellow-disciples would help you see how to move forward.

- As you did with your objectives, set a date for completion or reevaluation for each step toward your objective.

- The final part of this stage is the important subject of accountability. We're not on this journey alone and we all need help along the way. Sometimes we need a pat on the back (encouragement). Other times we need a kick in the rear (exhortation). With whom will you share these objectives so that they can regularly ask you helpful questions? This person should be willing to encourage you, pray for you regularly and push you when you need it. If you know who that is, write their name(s) here:

If you don't have this person, note 2 or 3 possible Barnabas-type folks who might encourage you on your journey. (Barnabas types encourage, exhort and stand up for us as well as stand up to us when we need it.) Make sure you ASK them!

Now, go back and look at each of your objectives, the steps toward them, and write down two or three actionable steps on each page. Then, if you're a list person, use this space to prioritize the most important steps here. It might be helpful to write a target date beside each step.

You're doing great!!!

Arguably, the next step is the most important.

7

PRAYING FORWARD

Move beyond plans into action!

Yes, praying is action, perhaps the most important action!

Each of your objectives deserve prayer. It doesn't matter what kind of objective it is, it is important for you to pray. Fill the following blank space with written prayers from and about your objectives.

Now that you're praying, write the names of your family on the left and then write a Scripture verse especially for them beside their name. Bible promises are especially good for this. This exercise will provide you with a list to pray biblical promises over your family. It will need updating as time goes by, so it will be helpful to begin a prayer journal to continue this process. Another helpful idea is to write 1-5 words next to each name to remind you how to intercede for the person you've written down.

Immediate family:

Other family, friends, colleagues and enemies (yes, let's pray for our enemies):

8

CELEBRATE

Congratulations!

The next step is to debrief.

If you're in a retreat or a guided session, the conversation with your facilitator may be an important next step. If you've done this on your own, well done!!

Display your objectives where you can see them regularly. Share those objectives with your spouse and others who are close to you. Ask them to hold you accountable. Put your goals in your calendar. Share your objectives with your fellow-disciples and ask them to pray for you and remind you that they are praying for your development.

Here are two last questions that may help you look forward:

What big thing would you like to focus on in the coming year?

What are some of the changes you would like to see in the next twelve months?

Again, Congratulations!

You have completed an important time of personal reflection. The purpose of this reflection is personal spiritual renewal. If we were sitting together in a retreat setting, you and I (and perhaps a small group of others) would get something to drink, sit and discuss our findings. One of my favorite questions to ask in one of these sessions is: "What surprised you as you thought, prayed and wrote your way through this time of reflection?" Then I would take a sip of coffee and wait for you to think about what may have surprised you. Based on your response, I would then turn to the section of A Fresh Start where you found this surprise and perhaps ask another question. As we go around the circle (if there is a circle), I would ask others similar questions. Before we completed our discussion, I would ask each person to share their four objectives and next action steps and ask who they will receive accountability from as they begin the journey toward those objectives. But you may be doing this alone. So, I would suggest that you take what you have decided and share it with your spouse and/or a friend. If that is not possible and you would like help, email me at info@ceokids.org. On the pages that follow are some resources to help you continue in your spiritual development.

> I hope that the result of this investment of time is just that,
> a fresh start. Press on!

PART THREE

9

SPIRITUAL DISCIPLINES

The disciplines (or practices) are an active means to abide in Christ. Through this abiding, He may use them to enliven and change our hearts and minds to be more like Him. The purpose of the disciplines is to grow in our knowledge and understanding of God and thus to be more faithful and fruitful followers of Jesus.

But **the disciplines are not an end unto themselves**. Their practice does not improve our standing with God, only the work of Jesus can do that. Each of us is different, and in that uniqueness, some disciplines are going to help you more than they might help me. But just because a discipline is not immediately profitable for you doesn't mean you should give up, you may profit from it later, so press on. Remember, the disciplines are not the way to get on God's 'good side', so forget that. **We use the disciplines to know Him better and through them, He may change us.**

The following descriptions of select disciplines is in alphabetical order so that one does not appear more important than another. They are written in a personal style as I share my own experience with them.

Finally, these are not laws or rules, there is no minimum daily requirement, but try some of them. As you're reading, use your pen to make some marks about the ones that resonate with you then practice a couple of them for a couple of weeks. Continue with the ones that nourish you and leave the others for another time.

Adoration Prayer
Adoration prayer expresses the awe I feel about God. It proclaim his greatness, remembers and expresses gratitude for his attributes (holiness, omnipresence, omnipotence, omniscience, justice, love and mercy, among others). Many have found that to dwell in this kind of prayer brings the praying person to a place of deep communion with and increased awe of God. The Psalms are full of adoration prayers. I've listed some Scripture in Chapter 1 that I use for this discipline. To simply pray the Bible is one of the easiest ways to begin the discipline of adoration praying. Slowly praying aloud Psalms 136 and 139 have been especially helpful to me for adoration prayer.

Bible Meditation
This is called Christian Meditation by some. I'm calling it Bible Meditation to contrast from other kinds of meditation (such as that practiced in Eastern religions and philosophies where emptying of one's mind is the focus). Jesus urged us to fill ourselves with Him, otherwise the Enemy will step in and fill the void. To dwell on a Scripture text through slow repetition as though I were trying to memorize it is an simple form of meditation. In doing such, I am slowing down, and dwelling carefully and intentionally on God's word. I also find that slowing copying a Bible text with a pen in a notebook is especially helpful as I focus my attention on God and His message for me.

Bible Memorization
When I was a high school Bible teacher, I had my students memorize Romans chapter twelve. Week after week they would be allowed five minutes to sit and study the verse of the week so that when called upon, they could write out that verse from memory. To focus on a passage and then to be able to recall that verse when least expected is a joyous thing. Some of the texts listed in Chapter 1 would be helpful verses to have memorized.

Bible Reading
To sit each morning and read and hear God's voice through his inspired word has several purposes: to know God better, to be changed by the words of God and to live a life that gives him glory because our thinking changes as we read. But, I think we must be sure that we are reading enough, too many people read far too little. These days I turn on the recorded reading of the Bible on my Bible app and listen as I read along. This slows me down and the practice allows my brain to receive through not just one, but two of my senses. I use a reading plan for my morning reading. I realized some time back that if left to my own choices, I would read too narrowly, and it is helpful to grow from the whole Bible. The YouVersion Bible app has many helpful plans and many translations. I use this and listen to the audio version of the Bible and read along. This is more slowly than a normal reading pace. Bible

reading should not be confused with Bible Study which is next.

Bible Study
When we want to know more about a Bible text, we study it. We look at the historical background of the book in question and then we look at the context of the verse(s) we are studying using a variety of study tools. We look for the original meaning of the author as inspired by the Holy Spirit so that we can properly understand and apply that truth to our life. Our goal of Bible study is growth in knowledge that leads to a growth in understanding that leads to a changed heart. Bible study is more intense and should not be confused with Bible reading.

Confession
It is important for me to name my sin every day and admit it to God. Without this naming and admission, repentance is very difficult. James instructs us to confess to one another. Jesus taught us to go to the offended brother, and then come to the altar. Making a regular practice of confession, to God and to one another will allow us to keep the Devil from using unconfessed sin against us. I find it helpful to have a written prayer of confession that I pray each morning (and/or each night). I also find it helpful to pause silently to consider which sin(s) of omission or commission needs to be confessed.

Disciple-making
The Great Commission has an imperative: "As you're going, make disciples". Making disciples is the process of walking together through life with other disciples, whom I call fellow-disciples (a small group of three is my ideal). By meeting regularly to encourage and exhort, we are able to urge one another forward, pointing one another to the gospel of Jesus. These meetings are regular (at least twice a month), vulnerable (a willingness to be truly open), and honest (without vulnerability, honesty will be too shallow to be meaningful). Ideally, these conversations are based on Scripture and prayer.
In the book, *As We're Going* I explore disciple-making historically, theologically and practically. Throughout that work and this book, I refer to meeting with fellow-disciples rather than suggesting one disciple is over another. Jesus is our master and we are fellow-disciples following him.

Evangelism
To decide to open our heart, mind and ears to those who have yet to meet Jesus is paramount to following him faithfully. Pray to become aware of those who need to hear the gospel, ask for the grace to go and speak the good news to them is our personal great commission.

Fasting
To give up food, TV, or -gasp- the Internet, is a helpful exercise to show us that God is god, instead of food, TV or the Internet. If I rely on anything more than I rely on God, I should think about doing without this thing for a period of time. One way to decide what may be the most important object of fasting would be to decide what is the thing you think you cannot do without. Then decide to do without it for a given period. One of the first lessons I learned about fasting from food was that I should have a specific matter to pray about. Then, during the fast, each time I felt hungry from not eating, I should pray about that matter.

Generosity
To give to the needs of others is a principle that is throughout the Bible. It is a way to learn to trust God. As we give away more of our resources, we are forced to rely on God more than on self.

Guidance
We all need guidance. It is essential for the follower of Jesus to find and walk together with fellow-disciples. But, often, this is not enough. It is wise to collaborate with a fellow disciple who has longer experience, knows how to listen, ask questions and is so devoted to the Lord that she/he may offer guidance for the life of a disciple. How often we speak with this fellow disciple will depend on their availability and our need. Sometimes we need more frequent conversations than others.

Holy Reading
I'm adapting this title from C. S. Lewis who referred to reading as important for growth (*Mere Christianity*). Indeed, to read that modern classic would be a great example of what I am calling holy reading. Well-chosen books about the Christian life are often helpful to the follower of Jesus. But all are not helpful. We would be wise to seek the counsel of those who have read more and for a longer period of time (this is where guidance can be important). The disciple of Jesus should not replace the regular reading of Scripture with reading books *about* the Bible. It is also noteworthy that Lewis advised that 1/3 of our reading should be at least 100 years old. He didn't want us to be caught up solely in the passing fancies of contemporary writers. There are many genres of holy reading. I suggest seeking a balance in: biography, books about the Bible (surveys, introductions and commentaries) and topical (this book is an example of the latter). To supplement our reading diet with C. S. Lewis will never hurt anyone. Please remember, reading books about the Bible should not replace reading the Bible itself.

Local Church Commitment
Every follower of Jesus needs to be in a community of fellow-disciples. This is essential to personal discipleship. To give glory to God through singing, Scripture reading, corporate intercession, expressing generosity, corporate confession, and being equipped by the preaching of the Bible are aspects of a local church gathering. The local church is also the body that prepares and sends ministers and fosters the planting of new churches worldwide. Every disciple of Jesus belongs in a local community of fellow-disciples. Disciple-making should flow out of the local church.

Prayer
Prayer is communicating with God. When I need to communicate with my wife, we talk face to face, by phone, and by other means. There are lots of methods to communicate with God. Indeed, in one way or another, all the disciplines are about communicating with God. We can train ourselves to carry on an almost constant conversation with God. This is the idea, I think, behind praying without ceasing. How glorious it is to realize, as C. S. Lewis taught, that I have God's complete attention because God has unlimited attention! But the main thing to remember is to talk to Him. And listen. So, the Bible is an essential tool for prayer. The old Adoration, Confession, Thanksgiving and Supplication form is a great way to pray.

Praying Into, and When Waking From Sleep
An influential leader once told me that there is a direct correlation between how I am sleeping and my current state of spiritual development. It made sense. So, I learned to break the Lord's Prayer into its phrases for use before I sleep. After I've said good night to my wife, I begin to practice adoration prayer. I talk with Him and reflect with my Heavenly Father about His greatness and His attributes. Reflecting on His goodness and power and being thankful are wonderful things to have on my mind as I drop off to sleep. He loves and cares for even a wretched sinner like me. What I've discovered is that once I've trained myself to do this as my last conscious communication before sleep, I sleep well. Then, when I awake, whether in the middle of the night or in the morning, I reenter this discipline of communicating with my Father in Heaven. When I've had occasion to teach this to others, they report that this practice has helped them sleep with more peace.

Psalmist (Scripture) Prayer
This was mentioned above as a method to practice adoration prayer. To use the Bible in prayer is to use God's own language in our conversation with Him. I have often referred to this practice as the steps that I climb that take me up to the throne of grace. There, I enjoy the presence of my heavenly

Father and make my requests to Him.

Reminders to Pray
This is an easier discipline. Choose five or six Scripture texts that you would like to regularly pray. Copy and paste these verses into your electronic calendar as reminders every hour or so through the day. As they pop up on your screen(s), take that moment, pause, and intentionally talk to your heavenly Father using that Bible text. There is a list you might find helpful to begin this process in Chapter 1.

Sabbath
This discipline was important enough to God for Him to model it on the 7th day and include it in the 10 Commandments. Among those commandments, this is likely the one most often ignored by Christians. To take a day off is biblical and wise. In a sermon on Sabbath, I could probably come up with lots of reasons why it's a good idea, but here are two: We need a day off because we were not created to work non-stop. God rested on the seventh day to demonstrate for us what He later commanded. The second reason is to show *me* that *I am not God* (like the need for sleep shows I need proper rest). Only God is all powerful. You and I need rest. But Sabbath is not just a day off. It should be intentional. Read the chapter on Sabbatical to adapt some ideas about purposeful Sabbath. Add an extra discipline or two to your sabbath. Be sure to engage in activities that bring you joy. Sabbath is to be enjoyed, not just endured! Oh, yeah, you pastors, Sunday is most likely *not* your sabbath.

Serving
If we run a search for the word 'serve' in the New Testament, it would take us quite a while to read the resulting list. (Reading and studying the uses of the word 'serve' in the Gospels may be a helpful thing to do as a Bible Study discipline.) Serving is a key to living the life of following Jesus. To serve well, it is important to identify and nurture the gifts and talents that God has given us. That, in itself is a lifelong discipline. However, it's important to be careful to understand that joyful serving comes from loving God first and serving out of that love. Serving for its own sake, or if motivated by guilt by another human, may lead into a works based religion filled with frustration and discouragement. As a fruit of abiding in Jesus, serving can bring us closer to those we serve and to God as we recognize it is him working through us, for his glory.

Silence
To be silent in today's world may be the most difficult, yet, perhaps, the most rewarding of the disciplines. This is simply not talking. When tempted

to talk, one should silently pray (perhaps a great place for adoration prayers). Like many such disciplines, to begin with a shorter period of time and then increase the amount of time is wise. In silence, one seeks to hear rather than to speak. This is not the same as an attempt to empty one's self, for any emptying of our heart and mind needs to be intentionally filled by God with His Scriptures. Silence may well be tied to one of the prayer disciplines. But, quietness so you can hear God is the key. Therefore, having your Bible open and ready is wise.

For God alone my soul waits in silence;
from him comes my salvation. (Psalm 62:1, ESV)

Simplicity
It is said that when Saint Augustine died, he had nothing but his writings and few clothes. Everything he had belonged to the monastery. To practice simplicity does not require a vow of poverty, but it does suggest moving away from a lifestyle that is focused on possessions into a lifestyle of less. Doing more with less means having fewer things around us to care for so that more of our attention may be toward God and people. If I didn't have to mow the lawn, that's forty minutes I could give to something else. But we must be careful about extremes. Because it is during that very forty minutes of mowing that I can often be in solitude and silence with God as I follow my noisy mower, oblivious to everything else, except the row of grass that I am cutting. It's about attitude, and asking: "Can I do without this thing?"

Singing
The Bible is filled with singing! To sing the praises of God is what many of the Psalms are all about. Singing is a form of worship (all of these disciplines may be seen as forms of worship). Whether alone in your prayer closet, or among your fellow-disciples, singing is a key discipline. On key, off key, whatever kind of joyful noise you can make, worship the Lord in singing! And don't think singing is just praise, we can lament in song as well, but in either case, rejoice always!

Solitude
Like silence, this may be difficult for some, especially the extrovert. But it is in being alone for a period of time that one may hear God and one's self. Solitude means to be alone and it goes naturally with silence. But unlike silence, you may not be silent, but instead be talking to God in prayer, praying aloud, or reading Scripture aloud. These may all be very meaningful aspects of solitude.

Submission
One does not have to join a religious order to practice submission. But I did have to make a commitment to some fellow-disciples to meet and be open to their input and challenges into my life. Practicing submission can be a simple as making myself accountable to a couple of fellow-disciples. They will care and ask me about my struggles and remind me of His grace. The better my brothers know me, the more I have confessed to them, the easier it will be for them to remind me that I am straying from the path that gives glory to God. Then I can submit to that counsel and turn back to my Lord.

Supplication
Supplication is an old English word that literally means begging earnestly with humility. It is often associated with asking for the needs of others, but as I'm using it, it is for our own needs also. When praying for others, it has often been called intercession. To practice supplication then, is to ask God for whatever is on my mind and heart. I would suggest this: Adore first, Confess humbly, Thank often and Supplicate last (ACTS). One more helpful practice is to keep a notebook where you list those requests. Then when each request is answered (in whatever way God chooses), write a prayer of thanksgiving beside or below it.

Thanksgiving
There is no question about the value of thanksgiving. This is true for the person expressing gratitude and the one receiving the thanks. Lots of studies show the value to our own well-being of be thankful. I have even found that it is helpful when I am struggling in a relationship with someone to practice thanking God for them as I pray for them. God uses that prayer to change my own heart toward them. But thanksgiving must also be directed toward God. If you're not sure that you have something to be thankful for, just thank God for your previous heartbeat and breath. To regularly practice the discipline of thanksgiving is as sure a path to change as one may take.

Writing
When we put our pen to paper to write, something happens in our brain to awaken it (apparently typing or reading don't have quite the same effect). When we intentionally write down Scripture, prayers and responses, we have slowed down the process and are paying more attention to those prayers and Scriptures. Therefore, copying Bible passages can make our prayer time more meaningful. (We've included several blank pages at the end of this book to give you space to begin this practice.) When I began to practice this discipline over twenty years ago, it was significant to my own personal renewal and ongoing spiritual development.

Next Steps:
Develop a plan for implementing some new disciplines. Perhaps you want to practice silence three times a week and an hour of solitude and silence once a week. The following table is a place to sketch a plan to get started.

	Make note of a discipline on the day(s) to practice it
Monday	
Tuesday	
Wednesday	
Thursday	
Friday	
Saturday	
Sunday	

~

Luther urged meditating daily on the Ten Commandments
and
using the Lord's Prayer as an outline for prayer.

10

BIBLE MEDITATION

The objective of Bible Meditation is to be filled, in contrast to much religious meditation that focuses on emptying. For the modern disciple, meditating on Scripture is not easy because it's not busy. Stop, focus and dwell on the Lord using His word.

I've been meditating on certain Scriptures for over a decade. Admittedly, it began as more reactive than proactive. I use Bible Meditation to return me to a focus on God when I naturally stray in focusing on the world. It is a means to capture worry and turn it into a prayer of faith. Today, it has become a daily practice that takes me deeper into the Bible that helps me grow in my understanding of God.

Process? Simple.

Identify Scriptures that lift you to Him.

Sit still, and SLOWLY read the text over and over (as though you were trying to memorize it - but just dwell, don't try to memorize, just linger over the text). If you're like a friend of mine you might pace around the room. I've been known to do this on the treadmill at the gym.

Don't study the text.

Just slowly read the text over and again. Ask your Father in Heaven to make the truth of the Bible clear to you as you read it.

For me, whenever I practice this, I am filled and encouraged. It will probably take you a few tries to figure out how this process works best for you, but key words are: quiet, focused, unhurried and listening. And don't give up too quickly, give the process a chance.

Below are three texts to get you started. (The list that begins on page 3 is a great resource for Bible meditation.)

"Set your minds on things that are above, not on things that are on earth." (Colossians 3:2)

"To you I lift up my eyes, O you who are enthroned in the heavens!" (Psalms 123:1

"Be exalted, O God, above the heavens! Let your glory be over all the earth!" (Psalms 57:5)

A practice that helps me build my list of Scripture is to pay attention to how Scripture speaks to me each day. I make note of it and add it to a document. This practice keeps my list fresh and growing.

We've included several blank pages at the end of this book where you might begin your own list.

11

SAILBOAT METAPHOR

The following four paragraphs give you something to consider in self-reflection. You may feel you are between one and another. That's okay. Their value is that they give a ready reference to track how you're doing on a regular basis. Having a working knowledge of these is particularly helpful in disciple-making conversations.

Am I Sailing?
Sailing is living the life of a disciple with the Spirit clearly filling my sails. I can feel the reality of God in my heart. I am aware of His presence. I see prayers answered. I can't wait to get into the Scripture, and when I do, I hear His voice speaking to me. He shows me through a variety of means that He is working in and through me to bless others. I can't wait to meet with fellow-disciples. It is easy to give Him all the glory. I am delighting in Him and through Him.

Am I Rowing?
Rowing means it feels more like a chore to sit down with God in the morning. I am being faithful to the disciplines of prayer and reading Scripture. But delighting in them seems more like a memory. I'm wrestling with some doubts and fears, but I am running to Him and trying to be patient. Even though I know prayers are being answered, I'm not recognizing it. But, no matter what, I will not give up. When I recognize that I'm feeling sorry for myself, I pray and press on. I'm working on my disciplines and letting my fellow-disciples know I'm struggling. I may not quite feel it, but I trust in God, who is with me.

Am I Drifting?
Just like rowing, I'm struggling with doubt and fear. But rather than being disciplined, I've just let go and sat back in the boat. I'm not only feeling sorry for myself, but I've slipped into behaviors that are harmful to me. I seek my identity or fulfilment, not in God, but in my job, food, sleep, TV, or whatever my favorite escape may be. I'm in the shadows and ignore God. I avoid my fellow-disciples, seeing their sin is easier than seeing my own.

Am I Sinking?
I have drifted into the dark. I feel no forward progress as a disciple of Jesus. The indifference and doubt has become cynicism – about Scripture, my fellow-disciples, even about God. My heart is more stone than flesh. I live in a swirl of self: pity, anger, unforgiveness, criticism and fear. I ignore calls from my fellow-disciples. I avoid community, because I see their hypocrisy more than my own. Were a tragic event to occur in my life right now, I might walk away from God altogether. My negligence overshadows my faith in God.

Don't Go It Alone, But Row!
It's hard to be a disciple, it's harder when I try alone. Focus on God through prayer and His word. Meet regularly with fellow-disciples. No matter what the circumstances, pray, keep the Scriptures open before you each morning, through the day, and meet regularly with fellow-disciples. Row. Row, even if you're pulling the oars and all you see is fog. Just keep rowing. Discipline really does lead to delight, so row. Through His word, through prayer and through my fellow-disciples, God will remind me again. The Spirit will blow, and I will begin to sail again. God is faithful. But no matter what, ROW![1]

---

[1] This metaphor is adapted from Tim Keller, *Prayer*, p. 258-259.

11

M'CHEYNE BIBLE READING PLAN

On the following pages you will find the M'Cheyne Bible Reading Plan. It takes you through the whole Bible, but as a bonus, takes you through the New Testament and Psalms twice.

M'Cheyne prepared this to be used in the morning and the evening. The first chapters in one's morning devotions, the second have as an evening household devotion.

Personally, I read the entire plan as the beginning of my daily disciplines each morning. I read expectantly, looking for a text or two that stands out. Then I reflect upon this passage, often copying in a notebook that I keep nearby (and posting on social media to encourage others with God's word).

Following the plan, we've left a few blank pages for such reflective activities as copying Scripture, making notes, writing prayers or whatever Spiritual Disciplines you decided to pursue. I might even take a knife and slice right through this book's spine at this point and put the plan and blank pages next to my Bible as a reminder to dig in. There's room to check each day and even to make a note or two. Don't see it as a job, dig in, so that it'll become a joy. Row that you may SAIL!!!

Gen 1, Matt 1, Ezra 1, Acts 1
Gen 2, Matt 2, Ezra 2, Acts 2
Gen 3, Matt 3, Ezra 3, Acts 3
Gen 4, Matt 4, Ezra 4, Acts 4
Gen 5, Matt 5, Ezra 5, Acts 5
Gen 6, Matt 6, Ezra 6, Acts 6
Gen 7, Matt 7, Ezra 7, Acts 7

Gen 8, Matt 8, Ezra 8, Acts 8
Gen 9-10, Matt 9, Ezra 9, Acts 9
Gen 11, Matt 10, Ezra 10, Acts 10
Gen 12, Matt 11, Neh 1, Acts 11
Gen 13, Matt 12, Neh 2, Acts 12
Gen 14, Matt 13, Neh 3, Acts 13
Gen 15, Matt 14, Neh 4, Acts 14

Gen 16, Matt 15, Neh 5, Acts 15
Gen 17, Matt 16, Neh 6, Acts 16
Gen 18, Matt 17, Neh 7, Acts 17
Gen 19, Matt 18, Neh 8, Acts 18
Gen 20, Matt 19, Neh 9, Acts 19
Gen 21, Matt 20, Neh 10, Acts 20
Gen 22, Matt 21, Neh 11, Acts 21

Gen 23, Matt 22, Neh 12, Acts 22
Gen 24, Matt 23, Neh 13, Acts 23
Gen 25, Matt 24, Est 1, Acts 24
Gen 26, Matt 25, Est 2, Acts 25
Gen 27, Matt 26, Est 3, Acts 26
Gen 28, Matt 27, Est 4, Acts 27
Gen 29, Matt 28, Est 5, Acts 28

Gen 30, Mark 1, Est 6, Rom 1
Gen 31, Mark 2, Est 7, Rom 2
Gen 32, Mark 3, Est 8, Rom 3
Gen 33, Mark 4, Est 9-10, Rom 4
Gen 34, Mark 5, Job 1, Rom 5
Gen 35-36, Mark 6, Job 2, Rom 6
Gen 37, Mark 7, Job 3, Rom 7

Gen 38, Mark 8, Job 4, Rom 8
Gen 39, Mark 9, Job 5, Rom 9
Gen 40, Mark 10, Job 6, Rom 10
Gen 41, Mark 11, Job 7, Rom 11
Gen 42, Mark 12, Job 8, Rom 12
Gen 43, Mark 13, Job 9, Rom 13
Gen 44, Mark 14, Job 10, Rom 14

Gen 45, Mark 15, Job 11, Rom 15
Gen 46, Mark 16, Job 12, Rom 16
Gen 47, Luk 1:1-38, Job 13, 1Co 1
Gen 48, Luk 1:39-80, Jo 14, 1Co 2
Gen 49, Luke 2, Job 15, 1 Cor 3
Gen 50, Luk 3, Job 16-17, 1 Cor 4
Ex 1, Luke 4, Job 18, 1 Cor 5

Ex 2, Luke 5, Job 19, 1 Cor 6
Ex 3, Luke 6, Job 20, 1 Cor 7
Ex 4, Luke 7, Job 21, 1 Cor 8
Ex 5, Luke 8, Job 22, 1 Cor 9
Ex 6, Luke 9, Job 23, 1 Cor 10
Ex 7, Luke 10, Job 24, 1 Cor 11
Ex 8, Luke 11, Job 25-26, 1Cor 12

Ex 9, Luke 12, Job 27, 1 Cor 13
Ex 10, Luke 13, Job 28, 1 Cor 14
Ex 11, Luke 14, Job 29, 1 Cor 15
Ex 12, Luke 15, Job 30, 1 Cor 16
Ex 13, Luke 16, Job 31, 2 Cor 1
Ex 14, Luke 17, Job 32, 2 Cor 2
Ex 15, Luke 18, Job 33, 2 Cor 3

Ex 16, Luke 19, Job 34, 2 Cor 4
Ex 17, Luke 20, Job 35, 2 Cor 5
Ex 18, Luke 21, Job 36, 2 Cor 6
Ex 19, Luke 22, Job 37, 2 Cor 7
Ex 20, Luke 23, Job 38, 2 Cor 8
Ex 21, Luke 24, Job 39, 2 Cor 9
Ex 22, John 1, Job 40, 2 Cor 10

Ex 23, John 2, Job 41, 2 Cor 11
Ex 24, John 3, Job 42, 2 Cor 12
Ex 25, John 4, Prov 1, 2 Cor 13
Ex 26, John 5, Prov 2, Gal 1
Ex 27, John 6, Prov 3, Gal 2
Ex 28, John 7, Prov 4, Gal 3
Ex 29, John 8, Prov 5, Gal 4

Ex 30, John 9, Prov 6, Gal 5
Ex 31, John 10, Prov 7, Gal 6
Ex 32, John 11, Prov 8, Eph 1
Ex 33, John 12, Prov 9, Eph 2
Ex 34, John 13, Prov 10, Eph 3
Ex 35, John 14, Prov 11, Eph 4
Ex 36, John 15, Prov 12, Eph 5

Ex 37, John 16, Prov 13, Eph 6
Ex 38, John 17, Prov 14, Phil 1
Ex 39, John 18, Prov 15, Phil 2
Ex 40, John 19, Prov 16, Phil 3
Lev 1, John 20, Prov 17, Phil 4
Lev 2-3, John 21, Prov 18, Col 1
Lev 4, Ps 1-2, Prov 19, Col 2

Lev 5, Ps 3-4, Prov 20, Col 3
Lev 6, Ps 5-6, Prov 21, Col 4
Lev 7, Ps 7-8, Prov 22, 1 Thes 1
Lev 8, Ps 9, Prov 23, 1 Thes 2
Lev 9, Ps 10, Prov 24, 1 Thes 3
Lev 10, Ps 11-12, Pro 25, 1Thes 4
Lev 11-12, Ps 13-14, Pr 26, 1Th 5

Lev 13, Ps 15-16, Pro 27, 2Thes 1
Lev 14, Ps 17, Prov 28, 2 Thes 2
Lev 15, Ps 18, Pro 29, 2 Thes 3
Lev 16, Ps 19, Pro 30, 1 Tim 1
Le 17, Ps 20-21, Pr 31, 1Tim 2
Lev 18, Ps 22, Eccl 1, 1 Tim 3
Lev 19, Ps 23-24, Ecc 2, 1Tim4

Lev 20, Ps 25, Eccl 3, 1 Tim 5
Lev 21, Ps 26-27, Ecc 4, 1Ti 6
Lev 22, Ps 28-29, Eccl 5, 2Ti 1
Lev 23, Ps 30, Eccl 6, 2 Tim 2
Lev 24, Ps 31, Eccl 7, 2 Tim 3
Lev 25, Ps 32, Eccl 8, 2 Tim 4
Lev 26, Ps 33, Eccl 9, Titus 1

Lev 27, Ps 34, Eccl 10, Titus 2
Num 1, Ps 35, Eccl 11, Titus 3
Num 2, Ps 36, Eccl 12, Phm 1
Num 3, Ps 37, Sng 1, Heb 1
Num 4, Ps 38, Sng 2, Heb 2
Num 5, Ps 39, Sng 3, Heb 3
Num 6, Ps 40-41, Sng 4, Heb 4

Num 7, Ps 42-43, Sng 5, Heb 5
Num 8, Ps 44, Sng 6, Heb 6
Num 9, Ps 45, Sng 7, Heb 7
Num 10, Ps 46-47, Sng 8, He 8
Num 11, Ps 48, Isa 1, Heb 9
Num 12-13, Ps 49, Isa 2, He 10
Num 14, Ps 50, Isa 3-4, Heb 11

Num 15, Ps 51, Isa 5, Heb 12
Num 16, Ps 52-54, Isa 6, He 13
Num 17-18, Ps 55, Isa 7, Jas 1
Num 19, Ps 56-57, Isa 8, Jas 2
Num 20, Ps 58-59, Isa 9, Jas 3
Num 21, Ps 60-61, Isa 10, Jas 4
Nu 22, Ps 62-63, Is 11-12, Ja 5

Num 23, Ps 64-65, Is 13, 1Pe 1
Num 24, Ps 66-67, Is 14, 1Pe 2
Num 25, Ps 68, Isa 15, 1 Pet 3
Num 26, Ps 69, Isa 16, 1 Pet 4
Num 27, Ps 70-71, Is17-18, 1Pe5
Num 28, Ps 72, Is 19-20, 2 Pet 1
Num 29, Ps 73, Isa 21, 2 Pet 2

Num 30, Ps 74, Isa 22, 2 Pet 3
Num 31, Ps 75-76, Isa 23, 1 Jn 1
Num 32, Ps 77, Isa 24, 1 Jn 2
Num 33, Ps 78:1-39, Is 25, 1 Jn 3
Num 34, Ps 78:40-72, Is 26, 1J 4
Num 35, Ps 79, Isa 27, 1 Jn 5
Num 36, Ps 80, Isa 28, 2 Jn 1

Deut 1, Ps 81-82, Isa 29, 3 Jn 1
Deut 2, Ps 83-84, Isa 30, Jude
Deut 3, Ps 85, Isa 31, Rev 1
Deut 4, Ps 86-87, Isa 32, Rev 2
Deut 5, Ps 88, Isa 33, Rev 3
Deut 6, Ps 89, Isa 34, Rev 4
Deut 7, Ps 90, Isa 35, Rev 5

Deut 8, Ps 91, Isa 36, Rev 6
Deut 9, Ps 92-93, Isa 37, Rev 7
Deut 10, Ps 94, Isa 38, Rev 8
Deut 11, Ps 95-96, Isa 39, Re 9
Deut 12, Ps 97-98, Is 40, Rev 10
Deut 13-4, Ps99-101, Is41, Re 11
Deut 15, Ps 102, Isa 42, Rev 12

Deut 16, Ps 103, Isa 43, Rev 13
Deut 17, Ps 104, Isa 44, Rev 14
Deut 18, Ps 105, Isa 45, Rev 15
Deut 19, Ps 106, Isa 46, Rev 16
Deut 20, Ps 107, Isa 47, Rev 17
Deut 21, Ps 108-109, Is 48, Re 18
Deut 22, Ps 110-111, Is 49, Re 19

Deut 23, Ps 112-113, Is 50, Re 20
Deut 24, Ps 114-115, Is 51, Re 21
Deut 25, Ps 116, Isa 52, Rev 22
Deut 26, Ps117-118, Is53, Matt 1
Deut 27, Ps 119:1-24, Is 54, Mat 2
Deut 28, Ps119:25-48, Is55, Mat 3
Deut 29, Ps119:49-72, Is56, Mat 4

Deut 30, Ps119:73-96, Is57, Mat 5
Deut 31, Ps119:97-120, Is58,Mat 6
Deut 32, Ps119:121-144, Is 59, Mat 7
Deut 33-34,Ps 119:145-176,Is 60, Mat 8
Josh 1, Ps 120-122, Is 61, Ma 9
Josh 2, Ps 123-125, Is 62, Ma 10
Josh 3, Ps 126-128, Is 63, Ma 11

Josh 4, Ps 129-131, Is 64, Ma 12
Josh 5, Ps 132-134, Is 65, Ma 13
Josh 6, Ps 135-136, Is 66, Mat 14
Josh 7, Ps 137-138, Jer 1, Ma 15
Josh 8, Ps 139, Jer 2, Matt 16
Josh 9, Ps 140-141, Jer 3, Mat 17
Josh 10, Ps 142-143, Jer 4, Ma 18

Josh 11, Ps 144, Jer 5, Matt 19
Josh 12-13, Ps 145, Jer 6, Mat 20
Josh14-15,Ps 146-147,Je 7,Ma 21
Josh 16-17, Ps 148, Jer 8, Mat 22
Josh18-19, Ps149-150, Je 9,Ma23
Josh 20-21, Acts 1, Jer 10, Mat 2
Josh 22, Acts 2, Jer 11, Matt 25

Josh 23, Acts 3, Jer 12, Matt 26
Josh 24, Acts 4, Jer 13, Matt 27
Judg 1, Acts 5, Jer 14, Matt 28
Judg 2, Acts 6, Jer 15, Mark 1
Judg 3, Acts 7, Jer 16, Mark 2
Judg 4, Acts 8, Jer 17, Mark 3
Judg 5, Acts 9, Jer 18, Mark 4

Judg 6, Acts 10, Jer 19, Mark 5
Judg 7, Acts 11, Jer 20, Mark 6
Judg 8, Acts 12, Jer 21, Mark 7
Judg 9, Acts 13, Jer 22, Mark 8
Judg 10, Acts 14, Jer 23, Mark 9
Judg 11, Act 15, Jer 24, Mar 10
Judg 12, Act 16, Jer 25, Mar 11

Judg 13, Act 17, Jer 26, Mar 12
Judg 14, Act 18, Jer 27, Mar 13
Judg 15, Acts 19, Je 28, Mar 14
Judg 16, Act 20, Je 29, Mar 15
Judg 17, Act21, Je30-31, Mar16
Judg 18, Acts 22, Jer 32, Luke 1
Judg 19, Acts 23, Jer 33, Luke 2

Judg 20, Acts 24, Jer 34, Luk 3
Judg 21, Acts 25, Jer 35, Luk 4
Ruth 1, Acts 26, Jer 36, Luke 5
Ruth 2, Acts 27, Jer 37, Luke 6
Rut 3-4, Act 28, Jer 38, Luke 7
1Sam 1, Rom 1, Jer 39, Luke 8
1Sam 2, Rom 2, Jer 40, Luke 9

1Sam 3, Rom 3, Jer 41, Luk 10
1Sam 4, Rom 4, Jer 42, Luk 11
1Sam5-6, Rom5, Jer 43, Luk12
1Sam7-8, Ro6, Jer44-45, Lu13
1Sam 9, Rom 7, Jer 46, Luk 14
1Sam 10, Rom 8, Je 47, Lu 15
1Sam 11, Rom 9, Jer 48, Lu 16

1Sam 12, Ro 10, Jer 49, Lu17
1Sam 13, Ro 11, Jer 50, Lu 18
1Sam 14, Ro 12, Je 51, Luk 19
1Sam 15, Ro 13, Je 52, Luk 20
1Sam 16, Ro 14, Lam 1, Lu 21
1Sam 17, Ro 15, Lam 2, Lu 22
1Sam 18, Ro 16, Lam 3, Lu 23

1Sam 19, 1Cor 1, La 4, Luk 24
1Sam 20, 1Cor 2, La 5, John 1
1Sam 21-22, 1Co 3, Eze 1, Joh 2
1Sam 23, 1Cor 4, Ezek 2, John 3
1Sam 24, 1Cor 5, Ezek 3, John 4
1Sam 25, 1Cor 6, Ezek 4, John 5
1Sam 26, 1Cor 7, Ezek 5, John 6

1Sam 27, 1Cor 8, Ezek 6, John 7
1Sam 28, 1 Cor 9, Ezek 7, Joh 8
1Sam 29-30, 1Cor 10, Ez 8, Jo 9
1Sam 31, 1Cor 11, Ez 9, Joh 10
2Sam 1, 1Cor 12, Ez 10, Jo 11
2Sam 2, 1Cor 13, Ez 11, Jo 12
2Sam 3, 1Cor 14, Ez 12, Jo 13

2Sam 4-5, 1Co 15, Ez 13, Jo 14
2Sam 6, 1Co 16, Ez 14, John 15
2Sam 7, 2Co 1, Ez 15, John 16
2Sam 8-9, 2Co 2, Ez 16, John 17
2Sam 10, 2Co 3, Ez 17, John 18
2Sam 11, 2Co 4, Ez 18, John 19
2Sam 12, 2Co 5, Ez 19, John 20

2Sam 13, 2Co 6, Ez 20, John 21
2Sam 14, 2Co 7, Ez 21, Ps 1-2
2Sam 15, 2Co 8, Ez 22, Ps 3-4
2Sam 16, 2Co 9, Ez 23, Ps 5-6
2Sam 17, 2Co 10, Ez 24, Ps 7-8
2Sam 18, 2Co 11, Ezek 25, Ps 9
2Sam 19, 2Co 12, Eze 26, Ps 10

2Sam 20, 2C 13, Ez 27, Ps11-12
2Sam 21, Ga 1, Eze 28, Ps 13-14
2Sam 22, Ga 2, Eze 29, Ps 15-16
2Sam 23, Gal 3, Eze 30, Ps 17
2Sam 24, Gal 4, Ezek 31, Ps 18
1Kgs 1, Gal 5, Ezek 32, Ps 19
1Kgs 2, Gal 6, Eze33, Ps 20-21

1Kgs 3, Eph 1, Ezek 34, Ps 22
1Kgs 4-5, Ep 2, Ez 35, Ps 23-24
1Kgs 6, Eph 3, Ezek 36, Ps 25
1Kgs 7, Ep 4, Ez 37, Ps 26-27
1Kgs 8, Ep 5, Ez 38, Ps 28-29
1Kgs 9, Eph 6, Ezek 39, Ps 30
1Kgs 10, Phil 1, Eze 40, Ps 31

1Kgs 11, Phil 2, Eze 41, Ps 32
1Kgs 12, Phil 3, Eze 42, Ps 33
1Kgs 13, Phil 4, Eze 43, Ps 34
1Kgs 14, Col 1, Eze 44, Ps 35
1Kgs 15, Col 2, Eze 45, Ps 36
1Kgs 16, Col 3, Eze 46, Ps 37
1Kgs 17, Col 4, Eze 47, Ps 38

1Kg 18, 1Thes 1, Ez 48, Ps 39
1Kg19, 1Ths2, Dan1, Ps40-41
1Kgs20, 1Ths3, Dan2, P42-43
1Kgs21, 1Thes4, Dan3, Ps 44
1Kgs 22, 1Thes 5, Dan 4, Ps 45
2Kgs 1, 2Ths 1, Da 5, Ps 46-47
2Kgs 2, 2Thes 2, Dan 6, Ps 48

2Kgs 3, 2Thes 3, Dan 7, Ps 49
2Kgs 4, 1Ti 1, Dan 8, Ps 50
2Kgs 5, 1Tim 2, Da 9, Ps 51
2Kgs 6, 1Ti 3, Da10, Ps52-54
2Kgs7, 1Ti 4, Dan 11, Ps 55
2Kgs 8, 1Ti5, Da12, Ps56-57
2Kgs 9, 1Ti6, Hos1, Ps58-59

2Kgs 10-11, 2T1, Ho2, P60-61
2Kgs 12, 2T2, Ho3-4, Ps62-63
2Kgs 13, 2Ti3, Ho5-6, P64-65
2Kgs 14, 2Ti4, Ho7, Ps66-67
2Kgs 15, Tit 1, Hos 8, Ps 68
2Kgs 16, Tit 2, Hos 9, Ps 69
2Kgs 17, Ti3, Ho10, Ps 70-71

2Kgs 18, Phm, Hos 11, Ps 72
2Kgs 19, Heb 1, Ho 12, Ps73
2Kgs 20, Heb 2, Ho13, Ps 74
2Kgs 21, He3, Ho14, Ps 75-76
2Kgs 22, He 4, Joel 1, Ps 77
2Kgs 23, Heb 5, Joe 2, Ps 78
2Kgs 24, He 6, Joel 3, Ps 79

2Kgs 25, He7, Amos 1, Ps80
1Chr 1-2,He 8,Am2,Ps81-82
1Chr 3-4,He9,Ams3,Ps83-84
1Chr 5-6,Heb10,Ams4,Ps 85
1Chr 7-8, Heb11, Ams 5, Ps86
1Chr 9-10, Heb12, Ams6, Ps 87-88
1Chr 11-12, He 13, Ams 7, Ps 89

1 Chr 13-14, Jas 1, Amos 8, Ps 90
1 Chr 15, Jas 2, Amos 9, Ps 91
1 Chr 16, Jas 3, Obad 1, Ps 92-93
1 Chr 17, Jas 4, Jonah 1, Ps 94
1 Chr 18, Jas 5, Jonah 2, Ps 95-96
1 Chr 19-20,1Pet 1, Jon 3,Ps97-98
1 Chr 21, 1Pet 2, Jon 4, Ps 99-101

1 Chr 22, 1 Pet 3, Mic 1, Ps 102
1 Chr 23, 1 Pet 4, Mic 2, Ps 103
1 Chr 24-25, 1Pet 5, Mic 3, Ps 104
1 Chr 26-27, 2Pet 1, Mic 4, Ps 105
1 Chr 28, 2 Pet 2, Mic 5, Ps 106
1 Chr 29, 2 Pet 3, Mic 6, Ps 107
2 Chr 1, 1 Jn 1, Mic 7, Ps 108-109

2 Chr 2,1Jn2, Nahum1, Ps 110-111
2 Chr 3-4, 1 Jn 3,Nah2,Ps 112-113
2 Chr 5, 1Jn 4, Nah 3, Ps 114-115
2 Chr 6, 1Jn 5, Hab 1, Ps 116
2 Chr 7, 2 Jn 1, Hab 2, Ps 117-118
2 Chr 8, 3 Jn 1, Hab 3, Ps 119:1-24
2 Chr 9, Jude, Zeph1, Ps 119:25-48

2 Chr 10, Rev1, Zep2, Ps 119:49-72
2 Chr 11-12,Rev2,Ze3,Ps119:73-96
2 Chr 13, Rev3,Hag1,Ps119:97-120
2 Chr 14-15,Re4,Ha2,Ps119:121-144
2 Chr 16,Re5,Zech1,Ps 119:145-176
2 Chr 17, Rev 6, Zech 2, Ps 120-122
2 Chr 18, Rev 7, Zech 3, Ps 123-125

2 Chr 19-20, Re 8, Ze 4, Ps 126-128
2 Chr 21, Rev 9, Zech 5, Ps 129-131
2 Chr 22-23,Rev10,Zec6,Ps132-134
2 Chr 24 ,Rev 11,Zec 7, Ps 135-136
2 Chr 25,Rev12, Zec 8, Ps 137-138
2 Chr 26, Rev 13, Zec 9, Ps 139
2 Chr 27-28,Re14,Zec10,Ps140-41

2 Chr 29, Rev 15, Zech 11, Ps 142
2 Chr 30, Rev 16, Zech 12, Ps 143
2 Chr 31, Rev 17, Zech 13, Ps 144
2 Chr 32, Rev 18, Zech 14, Ps 145
2 Chr 33, Re 19, Mal 1, Ps 146-147
2 Chr 34, Rev 20, Mal 2, Ps 148
2 Chr 35, Rev 21, Mal 3, Ps 149

2 Chr 36, Rev 22, Mal 4, Ps 150

The following pages are left blank for notes, copying Scripture, etc...

These pages are left blank for making notes, copying Scripture, etc…

These pages are left blank for making notes, copying Scripture, etc...

These pages are left blank for making notes, copying Scripture, etc...

These pages are left blank for making notes, copying Scripture, etc...

These pages are left blank for making notes, copying Scripture, etc…

These pages are left blank for making notes, copying Scripture, etc…

ABOUT CHRISTIAN EDUCATORS OUTREACH

*Extending Gospel Partnerships Worldwide through
Identifying, Training and Mentoring Leaders*

Christian Educators Outreach (CEO) is a not-for-profit, 501(c)(3) organization formed in the USA for spreading of the gospel of Jesus Christ through the support of partner organizations. CEO is qualified to receive tax deductible donations. As a not-for-profit organization, CEO relies on contributions that are solicited and received with the understanding that CEO maintains complete control over the use of donated funds and will be used for our mission.

Christian Educators Outreach
P.O. Box 6578
Charlottesville VA
22906

On our website, you can find more about our work, serving abroad with us, or joining us in financial partnership.

www.ceokids.org

Any proceeds from this resource go toward the funding of the ministry of Christian Educators Outreach.

ABOUT THE AUTHOR

Tom Foley has been married to Anna for more than forty years. They have two married daughters and are proud grandparents. He holds the Doctor of Ministry degree from Gordon-Conwell Theological Seminary and is founder and Executive Director of CEO. He travels internationally in a pastoral role serving Christian leaders, pastors, and missionaries. He loves taking photos in the places he visits, you can see lots of those pictures on his blog: www.kingdomtravelin.com, or on his Facebook or LinkedIn page. When he's not on a train or a plane, he is at home with Anna in Charlottesville. He has more of these resources in the works: a handbook for disciple makers, a book on leadership, and the story of the New Testament!

Made in the USA
Middletown, DE
07 September 2025

12821262R00056